My Senses
TASTING

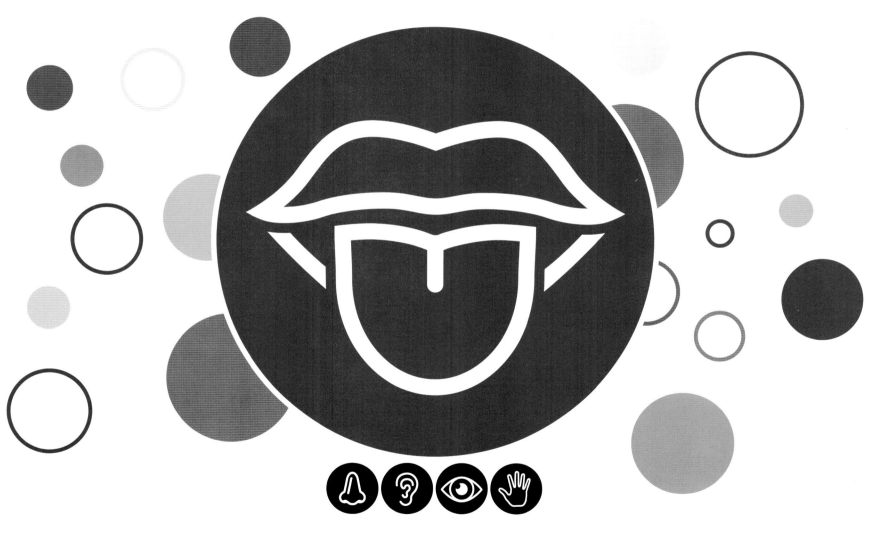

by
Grace Jones

Words written in **yellow** are explained in the glossary on page 24.

CONTENTS

©2016
Book Life
King's Lynn
Norfolk PE30 4LS

ISBN: 978-1-910512-68-5

Written by:
Grace Jones
Edited by:
Gemma McMullen
Designed by:
Drue Rintoul

A catalogue record for this book
is available from the British Library.

WHAT ARE MY SENSES?

We all have 5 **senses**. They are sight, smell, taste, touch and hearing.

Your senses tell you what is going on around you.

TONGUE

You use your tongue to taste the food you eat.

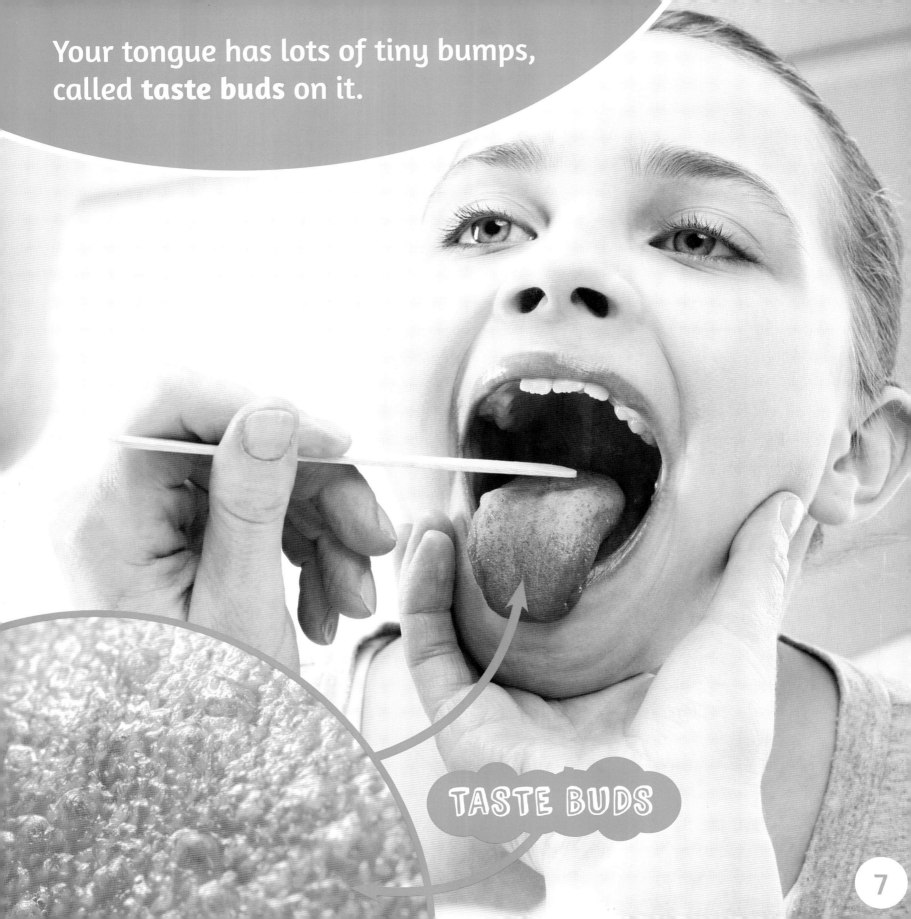

Your tongue has lots of tiny bumps, called **taste buds** on it.

TASTE BUDS

BRAIN

Special parts inside your taste buds send messages to your **brain**.

Your brain tells you what you are tasting.

There are many different tastes in the world,
these are called flavours.

10

There are four main flavours.
They are; sweet, sour, bitter and salty.

SWEET AND SOUR

Cakes, biscuits and ice cream taste sweet.

Lemons, rhubarb and pickles taste sour.

SOUR LEMONS

13

BITTER AND SALTY

Dark chocolate, celery and sprouts taste bitter.

Bacon, olives and seaweed taste salty.

SALTY BACON

AT THE SEASIDE

At the seaside, there is lots of tasty food to eat.

You can eat ice cream, fish and chips or even a stick of hard rock.

ICE CREAM

FISH AND CHIPS

STICKS OF ROCK

STAYING SAFE

Your sense of taste can tell you when a food is unsafe to eat.

When food has **gone off**
it has a bad taste.

SUPER SENSES!

BUTTERFLY

FEET

Butterflies use
their feet to taste with.

Some fish have taste buds on their bodies.

CATFISH

21

WHAT CAN YOU TASTE?

Find three foods with strong tastes and find a partner. Tell your partner to shut their eyes and get them to try a piece of each food.

Can they guess what each food is by its taste?

GLOSSARY

BRAIN
tells your body what to do.

GONE OFF
food that is old and unsafe to eat.

SENSES
tell you what is going on
around you.

TASTE BUDS
small bumps on your tongue which
let you taste.

INDEX